Speak the Word
Over Your Family
for Healing

by
Harry and Cheryl Salem

Speak the Word Over Your Family for Healing
ISBN 1-57794-344-9
Copyright © 2000 Salem Family Ministries
P.O. Box 701287
Tulsa, Ok. 74170

Published by Harrison House
P.O. Box 35035
Tulsa, Ok. 74153

Dedication

As a family we dedicate this healing book to our precious daughter, Gabrielle Christian Salem, our general and hero of faith. Gabrielle is the very best seed that we have and she has been planted into the greatest soil, Heaven. We expect an explosion of healing harvest in our lives and yours. Thank you, Gabrielle, you will always be the most precious gift that God has ever given us. We miss you terribly but will soon be together again forever . . .

Mom and Dad

List the names of the people you'll be praying for on this page.

_____

_____

_____

_____

_____

_____

_____

_____

_____

_____

_____

_____

_____

_____

_____

_____

_____

_____

_____

_____

_____

_____

Introduction

In our lives we have found that speaking the Word of God out loud changes our futures. It changes our families, our marriages, our hopes. Speaking the Word gives us faith, faith and confidence that God does what He says He will do.

The Lord said to us, "You think you have been praying My Word, but you have only been reading and saying My Word to me! I want you to write My Word out so that you can insert everyone's name into My Word. Then I want you to go down the list of all the people you are to pray for each day and individually pray, not just say the words but *pray*, with each person's name inserted right into My Word! Pray every word, My Word, out loud to Me. I will watch over it and perform it concerning the people whose names are inserted into

5

each prayer. You just activate My Word by praying it into the atmosphere."

Isaiah 44:26, "[The Lord] who confirms the word of His servant and performs the counsel of His messengers..." God listens to what we say and then He sends His messengers to perform what we say WHEN WE SAY WHAT HE SAYS!

Our job is to speak out of our mouths what God says and it is God's job to perform His Word when it is said into the atmosphere. God said to us, "You do what you are called to do and I will do what I am called to do."

We have seen many healings in our lives and many of them have been in our own bodies, minds, and emotions. We have learned the power of the spoken Word even in our own lives and families.

When I was eleven years old I was in an automobile accident that left me crippled with a short leg. I went through the windshield and had over one hundred stitches in my face. I was very careful when I found out that the words I speak have power, that my words spoken out of my mouth can truly affect my future.

I began to talk like I was already healed. I began to believe what I was saying. I began to act like what I was saying. Six years passed and my left leg was still shorter than my right leg. But I believed that God was already in the process of healing me so when the opportunity came for me to stretch my faith and believe God for a re-creative miracle, my confession had prepared my faith in advance.

On October twenty-first, 1974, I asked God to completely heal me and He did just that. My left leg grew out to be the same length as my right leg within just a few moments.

The scars on my face diminished little by little and today I can honestly say that I am the healed of the Lord. It is true. I am a miracle.

That was over twenty-five years ago.

There are many other miracles where the power of the spoken Word has brought the miraculous to reality. When I was pregnant with our third baby I hemorrhaged so badly the doctors told me that I had miscarried and that the baby was gone. I refused to believe this. I spoke Psalm 118:17 over myself and the baby in my womb, "This baby will live and not die and declare the works of the Lord in his/her life." Seven months later Gabrielle Christian Salem was born completely whole and healthy.

In 1992 depression tried to settle in my mind and emotions. With it came chronic fatigue syndrome, connective tissue disease, arthritis, and fibromialgia.

Through eighteen long, hard, and painful months I spoke God's healing words out loud every day over my own body. I am healed today and free from these horrible diseases because of the power of the spoken Word of God.

It's hard to imagine living our lives without the Word of God being spoken constantly in our home now. It has literally saved our lives and transformed our family.

Having had numerous miracles in my own life has made us know what to do when under attack of the enemy. It was the beginning of the New Year and there was excitement about God's blessings and promises to our family. We had just finished the most incredible year of our lives and the anticipation of the coming year was so exciting we could hardly wait!

The entire travelling schedule was already set on the calendar and we were ready to take God's Kingdom further than we had ever done before. We had been speaking the Word, praying in the Spirit, pleading the Blood of Jesus over each one of our families and ministry and we had begun to see positive effects from it all.

The week after Christmas we were in Mississippi with my family and we noticed that Gabrielle, our five-year old daughter, was having a problem sleeping. She would wake up screaming at the top of her lungs and no matter what we did nothing would calm her. Nightmares and night terrors plagued her night after night.

About a week later we were home and we noticed that her eyes were not moving properly. We first noticed it because she would turn her entire head to look at something instead of her eyes.

We began to try and get her to follow our finger with her eyes and she just couldn't do it. So we called our physician and explained what the symptoms were and he suggested we go and see an ophthalmologist. We made an appointment for the following Monday, January 11, 1999. We had no idea our entire world was about to be turned upside down!

The ophthalmologist examined our precious gift from God and told us the most devastating news we had ever heard before. The diagnosis was staggering. He immediately set up a MRI, called a specialist, and changed our world forever.

The report was evil. It was not from God therefore it had to have come from the devil. We had the wind knocked out of us from the start but we began to regroup and start warfare for our daughter's life.

The only defense we had was the Word of God. We had to resist the devil and this evil report. We had to speak what we know to be true and not what we were told or what we were seeing.

Remember the Bible says to "resist the devil and he will flee from you" James 4:7. The Word of God is not just defensive but it is also offensive warfare. God's Word protects us and it also helps us defeat the enemy with an offensive type weapon. We use it as a sword and a shield. The shield is protection and the sword defeats the devil and all his cohorts. This is the best way that we have found to resist the devil. Using the Word of God against the devil is truly resisting him!

As a family we immediately began to speak the Word of God concerning healing over Gabrielle. It was never easy but it was absolutely necessary to achieve the desired results we were after, HEALING! Harry would say over and over, "I'm not questioning God when it comes to healing, I'm counting on it."

It seemed like the longest road. There were days and opportunities that presented themselves that made us all want to quit, but there is no quitting when it comes to spiritual warfare. We are designed by God to always win if we will just stick with it until the victory comes from the supernatural to the natural realm. If we will resist the devil the unseen realm will literally swallow up the seen realm. What we see is not necessarily the truth. If the *seen* does not line up with God's Word, then we have a Bible right to believe God for the seen to be swallowed up by the *unseen*!

We believed God no matter what report the doctors gave us. We believed God no matter what the symptoms were. We believed God no matter what we felt. WE BELIEVED GOD! Months passed but time did not change the Word of God. It was still true. Each month we believed and expected the report of man to line up with the report of the Lord.

No matter what we asked God, no matter what the question was, God gave us the same answer every time. "I AM THE LORD THAT HEALS GABRI-ELLE. I WILL HAVE NO OTHER GODS BEFORE ME." It took us months before we realized the magnitude of those two statements. He was trying to get us to understand that no matter what we did in the natural, He must get the Glory. He must be glorified. He must be the One who heals her. We were to put no faith AT ALL, in anything or anybody other than God, her healer!

Little by little things were revealed to us that we had actually put faith in, med-icines, doctors, treatments, natural treat-ments, even faith in our faith! God said that He would have no other Gods before Him. We examined ourselves daily to make sure that all egos, pride, faith in anything or anybody other than God, our Father, was removed from our lives.

I am not saying that we didn't do anything to help aid in her healing. That would be ridiculous. The Amplified Bible says in Proverbs 18:9b, "...and he who does not use his endeavors to heal himself is brother to him who commits suicide." We searched for any information that could help. We read everything we could get our hands on. We prayed, confessed, believed, AND WORKED HARD to do all possible to help the situation. But it didn't take long to realize that all we could do was not worth much, EXCEPT SPEAK THE WORD OF GOD AND BELIEVE WHAT IT SAYS TO WORK FOR US IN THIS SITUATION!

We began to compile every scripture we knew on healing. We pulled out every old Bible we had used during different times in our lives when we needed healing. God had shown us and taught us many times before how to appropriate His Word to receive healing in our bodies, minds, and spirits. We knew that there were many scriptures already written out in the margins, underlined, and highlighted throughout all these Bibles.

Because of the revelation God had given us as a family about speaking the Word of God out loud we knew what we had to do. We were to take the Word of God concerning healing and we were to speak it out loud with Gabrielle's name right into the Word. We were to do it faithfully, daily, without question or hesitation.

We began with scriptures we had used to get healed before and as we read, studied, and prayed more and more scriptures have been revealed to us. You will find forty days of scripture to follow with blanks for the names of the people you are praying for who need healing in their lives. Take the Word of God like a prescription. Follow the directions, do not miss a dose, and continue until health has returned in full!

Remember God's Word says in Isaiah 55:11, "So shall my Word be that goes forth out of My mouth, it shall not return to Me void [without producing any effect, useless], but it shall accomplish that which I please and purpose, and it shall prosper in the thing for which I sent it." The word "prosper" in the Hebrew means to break through to success. The last part of that scripture would then literally read like this and I paraphrase "...but God's Word shall accomplish that which I please and purpose, and it shall break through to success in the thing for which I sent it."

God's Word will break through to success in our lives if we will say it. Psalm 107:20 says, "He sends forth His Word and heals them and rescues them from the pit and destruction." God gave His

Word to us and it is our job to send the Word through the air by speaking it out of our mouths. It's not enough to think it. We must speak it!

God showed us how to have creativity on this earth when He created it. He spoke everything into existence. He could have blinked it into existence, or thought it into existence, or any number or things but He *spoke* it into existence and that's how we must bring about the unseen into the seen realm, by speaking!

Jeremiah 1:12 says it best of all. "Then said the Lord to me, you have seen well, for I am alert and active, watching over My word to perform it."

God sees His Word. It is visible to Him. We think of words only being heard but in the case of God's Word being spoken it is seen and heard by God. Then He performs for us what He hears and sees us speak! So speak His Word and watch situations and circumstances change and rearrange.

This is what we have done over and over. We must not give in or give up. We must stay with it until we have won the victory. The Word of God works. All we have to do is say what It says and not what we want to say, or what we see.

Speak the Word of God over your self and your family over the next forty days and expect God to do what He says He will do. When you are finished with the forty days start over if you need to and do it again. Just don't stop or quit until you have the desired result you are after in your life and in the lives of your family. Believe that God's Word will work and it will!

One of the greatest promises that we have hung on to is in Numbers 23:19, "God is not a man, that He should tell or act a lie, neither the son of man, that He should feel repentance or compunction [for what He has promised]. Has He said and shall He not do it? Or has He spoken and shall He not make it good?"

When I saw this scripture the first five words jumped off the page at me and I meditated on them for weeks. "God is not a man...". I would say over and over, "God is not a man, God is not a man, God is not a man..."

It took me a while but I finally got the full impact of what the Father God wanted me to see. GOD IS NOT A MAN!!! HE IS GOD AND GOD ALONE!!!

I got it. Did you? Don't look at God like we do to people to keep their word. God is God and He does not lie. He does not promise something and then not keep that promise. That's why as you speak the Word over yourself and your family for healing, remember these are God's promises and He does not lie. He performs what He says when we SAY WHAT HE SAYS!

Gabrielle was the most prayed for little girl in the world. Not only were we speaking the Word and believing God for her healing but countless others were praying also. Each month her symptoms were worse but we never wavered.

God was showing us so many revelations and one was that many times people make "death" the healer. God continued to say to us "I am the Lord that heals her. You will have no other gods before Me."

We refused to let death be her healer and one day we realized this was one of satan's greatest deceptions. When death becomes a healer in our minds then death becomes a god. We must hold our ground and if healing comes in crossing over to the other side instead of healing on the earth we must be very careful not to fall into the mental trap of calling "death" the healer.

On November 23, 1999 Gabrielle crossed over. She went beyond the veil but death did not take her. Death did not heal her. We walked her as far as we could on this side of the valley of the shadow of death. The angels came three times throughout the night to take her, but we continued to speak life and the angels would back off. Finally, at seven a.m. Jesus Himself came and she ran so fast into His arms that she left her sick body behind. It was easy and quick and Jesus remained the healer, not death.

It wasn't the desired result we wanted or anticipated but when confronted with other situations where healing is needed we will always do it the same way. We spoke life over and over and ultimately life came, more life than we truly can imagine. Gabrielle truly has life, more life than we have on this earth.

The Word works when we work the Word of God. There is no doubting the restorative power of this incredible healing. No, it was not what we wanted but it does not change our faith or our trust in our Father God. Nor does it change the Word of God.

We speak the Word of God continually out loud and expect God to perform His Word. Whether we like it or not, that's exactly what He did, His way, not ours. We may never understand as long as we are on this earth but we completely and totally trust God. We will continue to do it the same way over and over again because God is not a man that He should lie!

Day One
Galatians 3:13

Christ purchased _____'s freedom [r e d e e m i n g _____] from every curse (doom) of the Law [and its condemnation] by [Himself] becoming a curse for _____, for it is written [in the Scriptures], Cursed is everyone who hangs on a tree (is crucified).

Isaiah 53:5

But He was wounded for _____'s transgressions, He was bruised for _____'s guilt and iniquities; the chastisement [needful to obtain] peace and well-being for _____ was upon Him, and with the stripes [that wounded] Him _____ is healed and made whole.

A place for your thoughts.

_____

_____

_____

_____

_____

_____

_____

_____

_____

_____

_____

_____

_____

_____

_____

_____

_____

_____

_____

_____

_____

_____

_____

_____

_____

_____

Day Two
I Peter 2:24

> He personally bore _____'s sins in His [own] body on the tree [as on an altar and offered Himself on it], that _____ might die (cease to exist) to sin and live

to righteousness. By His wounds _____ has been healed.

III John 2

Beloved, I pray that _____ may prosper in every way and [that _____'s body] may keep well, even as [I know] _____'s soul keeps well and prospers.

Place your prayer thoughts here.

_____

_____

_____

_____

_____

_____

_____

_____

_____

_____

_____

_____

_____

_____

_____

_____

_____

_____

_____

_____

_____

_____

_____

_____

_____

_____

_____

_____

Day Three
Jeremiah 29:11

For I know the thoughts and plans that I have for _____, says the Lord, thoughts and plans for welfare and peace and not for evil, to give _____ hope in _____'s final outcome.

Psalm 91:11

For He will give His angels charge over _____ to accompany and defend and preserve _____ in all _____'s ways [of obedience and service].

Pray and journal.

_____

_____

_____

_____

_____

_____

For with God nothing is ever impossible and no Word from God shall be without power or impossible of fulfillment for _____.

Day Four
Luke 1:37

Proverbs 18:21

Death and life are in the power of the tongue, and _____ who indulges in it shall eat the fruit of it [for death or life].

Proverbs 12:18

There are those who speak rashly, like the piercing of a sword, but the tongue of the wise brings healing for _____.

Write your thoughts.

_____

_____

_____

_____

_____
_____
_____
_____
_____
_____
_____
_____
_____
_____
_____
_____
_____
_____
_____
_____
_____
_____
_____
_____
_____
_____
_____
_____
_____
_____

Truly I say to
_____, if
_____ has
faith [that is living]
like a mustard seed,
_____ can say
to this mountain,
Move from here to
yonder place, and it will move; and nothing will be impossible to _____.

Day Five
Matthew 17:20b

Philippians 4:13

_____ has strength for all things
in Christ Who empowers _____
[_____ is ready for anything and equal
to anything through Him Who infuses
inner strength into _____; _____ is
self-sufficient in Christ's sufficiency].

Don't forget to pray!

_____

_____

_____

_____

Day Six
John 3:16

For God so greatly loved and dearly prized _____ that He [even] gave up His only begotten (unique) Son, so that whoever believes in (trusts in, clings to, relies on) Him shall not perish (come to destruction, be lost) but have eternal (everlasting) life.

Matthew 15:13b

...Every plant which My Heavenly Father has not planted in _____ will be torn up by the roots.

Remember God watches over His Word!

_____
_____
_____
_____
_____

Then _____ will call upon God and _____ will come and pray to God, and God will hear and heed _____. Then _____ will seek God, inquire for, and require God as a vital necessity and find God when _____ searches for God with all (his, her) heart. I will be found by _____, says the Lord, and I will release _____ from captivity, and gather _____ from all the nations, and all the places to which I have driven _____, says the Lord, and I will bring _____ back to the place from which I caused _____ to be carried away captive.

Day Seven
Jeremiah 29:12-14

Speak God's Word out loud!

_____

_____

_____

_____

_____

Day Eight
Proverbs 10:22

_____ walks in the blessing of the Lord — it makes _____ truly rich, and God adds no sorrow with it (neither does toiling increase it.)

Proverbs 3:2

For length of days and years of a life [worth living] and tranquility [inward and outward and continuing through old age till death]; these shall they add to _____.

God is listening. Keep praying.

_____
_____
_____
_____
_____
_____
_____

For the Lord God helps _____; therefore has _____ not been ashamed or confounded. Therefore, has _____ set (his, her) face like a flint, and _____ knows that (he, she) shall not be put to shame.

Day Nine
Isaiah 50:7

(*Author's note: This was written as prophesy for Jesus but because we are engrafted into Him, what was His is now ours!)

Isaiah 51:16a

And I have put My Words in _____'s mouth and have covered _____ with the shadow of My hand... says the Lord to _____.

Pray and journal.

_____

_____

_____

_____

_____

_____

_____

_____

_____

_____

_____

_____

_____

_____

_____

_____

_____

_____

_____

_____

_____

_____

_____

_____

_____

_____

_____

_____

My child, attend to My Words; consent and submit to My sayings. Let them not depart from _____'s sight; keep them in the center of _____'s heart. For they are life to _____ who finds them, healing and health to all _____'s flesh.

Day Ten
Proverbs 4:20-22

Jeremiah 30:17a

For God will restore health to _____, and God will heal _____'s wounds...

Jeremiah 33:3a

Call to Me and I will answer _____ and show _____ great and mighty things, fenced in and hidden...

Don't forget to journal!

_____

_____

Speak the Word Over Your Family

_____
_____
_____
_____
_____
_____
_____
_____
_____
_____
_____
_____
_____
_____
_____
_____
_____
_____
_____
_____
_____
_____
_____

He Himself took [in order to carry away] _____'s weaknesses and infirmities and bore away _____'s sicknesses.

Day Eleven
Matthew 8:17

Psalm 57:1,2

Be merciful and gracious to _____, O God, be merciful and gracious to _____, for _____'s soul takes refuge and finds shelter and confidence in You; yes, in the shadow of Your wings will _____ take refuge and be confident [until calamities and destructive storms are passed].

_____ will cry to God Most High, Who performs on _____'s behalf and rewards _____ [Who brings to pass His purposes for _____ and surely completes them]!

_____

_____

_____

_____

_____

_____

_____

_____

_____

_____

_____

_____

_____

_____

_____

_____

_____

_____

_____

_____

_____

_____

_____

_____

_____

_____ will keep and guard (his, her) heart with all vigilance and above all that _____ guards, for out of it flows the springs of life.

Day Twelve
Proverbs 4:23

I John 4:4

Little child, _____ is of God [_____ belongs to Him] and has [already] defeated and overcome them [the agents of the antichrist], because He Who lives in _____ is greater (mightier) than he who is in the world.

Pray and write your thoughts.

_____

_____

_____

_____

_____

_____

_____

Day Thirteen
John 10:29

My Father, Who has given _____ to Me, is greater and mightier than all [else]; and no one is able to snatch [_____] out of My hand, says Jesus.

Malachi 3:10-11a

_____ will bring all the tithes into the storehouse, that there may be food in My house, and prove Me now by it, says the Lord of hosts, if I will not open the windows of heaven for _____ and pour out a blessing, that there shall not be room enough to receive it. And I will rebuke the devourer [insects and plagues] for _____'s sake and the devourer shall not destroy the fruits of _____'s ground.

Pray and journal.

_____

_____

_____

_____

_____

_____

_____

_____

_____

_____

_____

_____

_____

_____

_____

_____

_____

_____

_____

_____

_____

_____

_____

_____

_____

Day Fourteen
Psalm 27:1-3

The Lord is _____'s Light and _____'s Salvation. Whom shall _____ fear? The Lord is the Refuge and Stronghold of _____'s life. Of whom shall _____ be afraid? When the wicked, even _____'s enemies and _____'s foes, came upon _____ to eat up _____'s flesh, they stumbled and fell. Though a host encamp against _____, _____'s heart shall not fear; though war arise against _____ [even then] in this will _____ be confident.

Ask God for insight and revelation as you pray.

_____
_____
_____
_____
_____
_____

But know that the
Lord has set apart for
Himself [and given
distinction   to]
_____ who is
godly [_____ who
is of loving-kindness].
The Lord listens and
heeds when _____ calls to Him.

Day Fifteen
Psalm 4:3

II Chronicles 7:14

If _____, who is called by Christ's
name, will humble him/herself, pray,
seek, crave and require of necessity the
Lord's face and turn from all wicked
ways, then will I hear from heaven, for-
give their sin, and heal _____'s land.
("Land" is representative of who you are,
of your heritage, your family.)

*What is God telling you? Write it
down.*

_____

_____

_____

_____

_____

_____

_____

_____

_____

_____

_____

_____

_____

_____

_____

_____

_____

_____

_____

_____

_____

_____

_____

_____

_____

_____

_____

The steps of _____ are directed and established by the Lord when _____ delights in the Lord's way [and the Lord busies Himself with _____'s every step].

Day Sixteen
Psalm 37:23

Acts 2:28

You have made known to _____ the ways of life; You will enrapture _____ [diffusing _____'s soul with joy] with and in Your presence.

Journal your thoughts.

_____

_____

_____

_____

_____

_____

_____

_____

Day Seventeen
Psalm 103:1-5

Bless (affectionately, gratefully praise) the Lord, O _____'s soul; and all that is [deepest] within _____, bless His holy name! Bless the Lord, O _____'s soul, and forget not [one of] all His benefits, Who forgives [every one of] all _____'s iniquities, Who heals [each one of] all _____'s diseases, Who redeems _____'s life from the pit and corruption, Who beautifies, dignifies, and crowns _____ with lovingkindness and tender mercy; Who satisfies _____'s mouth [_____'s necessity and desire at _____'s personal age and situation] with good so that _____'s youth, renewed, is like the eagle's [strong, overcoming, soaring]!

_____

_____

_____

Day Eighteen
II Corinthians
2:14

But thanks be to God, Who in Christ always leads _____ in triumph [as trophies of Christ's victory] and through _____ spreads and makes evident the fragrance of the knowledge of God everywhere.

Job 33:4

[It is] the Spirit of God that has made _____ [which has stirred _____ up]; the breath of the Almighty gives _____ life [which inspires _____].

Pray and ask God for revelation.

_____

_____

_____

_____

_____

_____

Surely or only goodness, mercy, and unfailing love shall shall follow _____ all the days of _____'s life, and through the length of _____'s days the house of the Lord [and His presence] shall be _____'s dwelling place..

Day Nineteen
Psalm 23:6

Psalm 20:5

We will [shout in] triumph at _____'s salvation and victory, and in the name of our God we will set up our banners. May the Lord fulfill all _____'s petitions.

Pray in your prayer language!

_____
_____
_____
_____
_____

Day Twenty
Psalm 20:1-4

May the Lord answer _____ in the day of trouble! May the name of the God of Jacob set _____ up on high [and defend _____].

(May the Lord) send _____ help from the sanctuary and support, refresh, and strengthen _____ from Zion; Remember all _____'s offerings and accept _____'s burnt sacrifice [Selah: pause and think of that!] May God grant _____ according to (his, her) heart's desire and fulfill all (his, her) plans.

Selah really means to pause and think so this is a perfect time to "selah"!

Now I know that the Lord saves _____, His anointed; He will answer _____ from His holy Heaven with the saving strength of His right Hand. Some trust in and boast of chariots and some of horses but _____ trusts in and boasts of the name of the Lord our God. They are bowed down and fallen but _____ is risen and stands upright. O Lord, give victory to _____; let the King answer _____ when (he, she) calls.

Day Twenty-one
Psalm 20:6-9

Ask God for wisdom when you pray.

_____
_____
_____
_____
_____
_____
_____

Day Twenty-two

Proverbs 3: 4-8

So shall _____ find favor, good understanding, and high esteem in the sight (or judgement) of God and man. _____ will lean on, trust in, and be confident in the Lord with all (his, her) heart, and mind, and _____ will not rely on (his, her) own insight and understanding. In all _____'s ways (he, she) knows, recognizes, and acknowledges God, and God will direct and make straight and plain _____'s paths. _____ is not wise in (his, her) own eyes; reverently fearing and worshiping the Lord, and _____ turns entirely away from evil. The Word of God shall be health to _____'s nerves, and sinews, and marrow, and moistening to _____'s bones.

Pray, listen, and write.

_____

_____

_____
_____
_____
_____
_____
_____
_____
_____
_____
_____
_____
_____
_____
_____
_____
_____
_____
_____
_____
_____
_____
_____
_____
_____

Day Twenty-three
Isaiah 49:23b, 25b

...For _____ shall not be put to shame who waits for, looks for, hopes for, and expects God.

For God will contend with him who contends with _____, and God will give safety to _____'s children and ease them.

Psalm 138:8

The Lord will perfect that which concerns _____, Your mercy and loving kindness, O Lord, endure forever. Thank You, Lord that You do not forsake the works of Your own hands concerning _____.

Pray in the Spirit of God.

_____

_____

_____

Speak the Word Over Your Family

_____

_____

_____

_____

_____

_____

_____

_____

_____

_____

_____

_____

_____

_____

_____

_____

_____

_____

_____

_____

_____

_____

_____

_____

57

Day Twenty-four
Exodus 23:25

_____ shall serve the Lord (his, her) God; He shall bless _____'s bread and water, and I will take sickness from _____'s midst.

II Corinthians 1:11

[The lips of] many persons [turned toward God will eventually] give thanks on _____'s behalf for the (blessing of deliverance) granted _____ at the request of the many who have prayed.

I John 5:4

For _____ is born of God and is victorious over the world; and this is the victory that conquers the world even our faith.

Pray and write.

_____

_____

_____

_____

_____

_____

_____

_____

_____

_____

_____

_____

_____

_____

_____

_____

_____

_____

_____

_____

_____

_____

Day Twenty-five | _____ will
Hebrews 12:1-2b | run with patient endurance the appointed course of the race set before (him, her) looking away [from all that will distract] to Jesus, who is the Leader and the Source of (his, her) faith and is also, it's finisher [bringing it to perfection].

Psalm 32:7

God, You are _____'s hiding place, and You will protect _____ from trouble, and surround _____ with songs of deliverance.

Romans 16:20

And the God of Peace will soon crush satan under _____'s feet.

Seek God's face today.

_____

_____

_____

_____

_____

_____

_____

_____

_____

_____

_____

_____

_____

_____

_____

_____

_____

_____

_____

_____

_____

Day Twenty-six
Joshua 21:45

Not a word failed of any good thing which the Lord had spoken (for _____)... all came to pass (for _____).

Philippians 2:13

For it is God who works in _____ both to will and to do for His good pleasure.

Revelations 12:11

And _____ overcame the devil (and sickness) because of the blood of the Lamb, and because of the Word of (his, her) testimony.

God wants to give you insight. Write it down!

_____
_____
_____
_____

_____

_____

_____

_____

_____

_____

_____

_____

_____

_____

_____

_____

_____

_____

_____

_____

_____

_____

_____

_____

_____

_____

_____

Day Twenty-seven

Hebrews 4:14, 16

_____ will hold fast to (his, her) confession of faith concerning all of God's promises in Christ. Let _____ then fearlessly and confidently and boldly draw near to the throne of grace, the throne of God's unmerited favor to _____, that _____ may receive mercy...

Romans 8:11

He who raised Christ from the dead will also give life to _____'s mortal body through His Spirit who dwells in _____.

II Corinthians 1:20

For all the promises of God are yes, and in Him, Amen, to the glory of God through _____.

It's time for warfare prayer!

_____

_____

_____

_____

_____

_____

_____

_____

_____

_____

_____

_____

_____

_____

_____

_____

_____

_____

_____

_____

_____

Day Twenty-
eight
Matthew 8:2,3

I thank You, Lord,
that You are willing to
heal _____ and to
make (him, her) clean.

Exodus   15:26

_____ will dili-
gently heed the voice
of the Lord (his, her) God and will do
what is right in His sight, _____ will
give ear to His commandments and keep
all His statutes, God will put none of the
diseases on _____ which He allowed
to be put on the Egyptians. For God is the
Lord who heals _____.

Speak God's Word. He is listening.

_____
_____
_____
_____
_____
_____
_____

God is a rewarder of _____ who diligently seeks Him.

Day Twenty-nine
Hebrews 11:6

Deuteronomy 7:15

And the Lord will take away from _____ all sickness and will afflict _____ with none of the terrible diseases of Egypt which _____ has known about (* under the curse in Deuteronomy 28), but will lay them on those who hate _____.

Psalm 91:16

With long life will I satisfy _____, and show _____ My salvation.

Pray and journal!

_____
_____
_____
_____
_____

God sent His Word and healed _____, and delivered _____ from the pit and destruction.

Psalm 118:17

_____ shall not die, but live, and declare the works of the Lord in (his, her) life.

Jeremiah 30:17

For I will restore health to _____ and heal _____ of (his, her) wounds.

God wants to speak to you, just listen.

_____
_____
_____
_____
_____
_____

Day Thirty-one
Matthew 18:18

Assuredly, I say to you, whatever _____ binds on earth will be bound in heaven, and whatever _____ looses on earth will be loosed in Heaven. We loose healing in _____'s life in Jesus name. We bind sickness, disease, infirmity, and every evil report from the enemy in Jesus name in _____'s life.

Matthew 18:19

Again, I say to _____ that if two of you shall agree on earth concerning anything that we may ask (concerning _____) it will be done for _____ by Our Father in Heaven.

God is for you and He agrees with you concerning His own Word!

_____

_____

_____

_____

_____

_____

_____

_____

_____

_____

_____

_____

_____

_____

_____

_____

_____

_____

_____

_____

_____

_____

_____

_____

_____

_____

_____

Day Thirty-two | _____ has
Mark 11:22-24 | faith in God. For
| assuredly, I say to
| _____, whoever
| says to this mountain
| (* name the problem),
| "Be removed and be
| cast into the sea," and
we do not doubt in our hearts but we
believe that those things that we say will
come to pass, we will have whatever we
say concerning healing for _____.
Therefore I say to _____, whatever
things we ask when we pray, we believe
that we receive them and we will have
them (concerning _____'s healing).

*We speak the Word and God per-
forms the Word.*

We are wor-shipers of God and we do God's will, and God hears us con-cerning all our requests for _____'s healing

Day Thirty-three
John 9:31

John 10:10

The thief does not come except to steal, and to kill, and to destroy. Jesus has come that _____ may have life and that _____ may have it more abundantly. Therefore, we call upon the name of the Lord Jesus that _____ has life and that (he, she) has it more abundantly.

Hebrews 10:23

Let _____ hold fast the confession of (his, her) hope (faith) without waver-ing for God promised and He is faithful.

_____

_____

_____

_____

_____

_____

_____

_____

_____

_____

_____

_____

_____

_____

_____

_____

_____

_____

_____

_____

_____

_____

And these signs shall follow those who believe, (and we believe!)... we shall lay hands on _____, and _____ will recover.

Day Thirty-four
Mark 16:17,18

Hebrews 10:35

Therefore, _____ does not cast away (his, her) confidence, which has great reward.

Hebrews 13:8

Jesus Christ is the same yesterday, today, and forever...(concerning _____'s healing.

Pray and watch the anointing of God pour over this situation!

_____
_____
_____
_____

_____
_____
_____
_____
_____
_____
_____
_____
_____
_____
_____
_____
_____
_____
_____
_____
_____
_____
_____
_____
_____
_____
_____
_____
_____
_____

Let the weak say "I am strong." Therefore we say that _____ is now strong in Jesus' name!

James 5:14,15

Day Thirty-five
Joel 3:10

Is anyone among you sick? Let _____ call for the elders of the church, and let them pray over _____, anointing _____ with oil in the name of the Lord. And the prayer of faith will save the sick, and the Lord will raise _____ up. And if _____ has committed sins, _____ will be forgiven.

Isn't it wonderful to know that God listens and He answers! Write your thoughts.

_____

_____

_____

_____

_____

Day Thirty-six
Isaiah 43:25,26

God says, "I, even I, am He who blots out _____'s transgressions for My own sake, and I will not remember _____'s sins. Put Me in remembrance; let us contend together; state your case, that _____ may be acquitted." We state our case before You, Lord, and we thank You that Your Word is true and that we can stand upon it and rely upon it. We thank You, that You mean what You say and You say what You mean. We thank You that healing is our heritage, and that _____ will live a long and healthy life in Jesus name. We thank You that You are what You say and You say what you are, I AM THAT I AM!

God is not a man that He should lie. Write your thoughts as you pray.

_____

_____

_____

_____

_____

_____

_____

_____

_____

_____

_____

_____

_____

_____

_____

_____

_____

_____

_____

_____

_____

_____

_____

_____

Day Thirty-
seven
I John 5:14,15

Now this is the confidence that _____ has in Christ, that if _____ asks anything according to God's will, He hears (him, her). And if _____ knows that God hears (him, her), whatever _____ asks, _____ knows that (he, she) has the petitions that (he, she) has asked of Him.

I John 3:21,22

Beloved, if _____'s heart does not condemn (him, her), _____ has confidence toward God. And whatever _____ asks (he, she) receives from Christ, because _____ keeps His commandments and does those things that are pleasing in His sight.

_____

_____

_____

_____
_____
_____
_____
_____
_____
_____
_____
_____
_____
_____
_____
_____
_____
_____
_____
_____
_____
_____
_____
_____
_____
_____
_____

Day Thirty-
eight
Nahum 1:9

Affliction will not rise up against _____ a second time. (*Because Jesus went to Calvary and took stripes on His back and took all of our sicknesses and diseases to the cross, *that* was the first time for us. So, it has no right to us *now* [the second time] which is the first time we experience it. Nahum did not have what we have through Christ. Christ took it for us the first time AND it has no right to rise up 'a second time' against us. So it has no right to us at all! Glory to God!)

Pray and write what God is saying.

_____

_____

_____

_____

_____

_____

_____

For the weapons of _____'s warfare are not carnal, but mighty through God to the pulling down of strongholds; _____ casting down imaginations, and every high thing that exalts itself against the knowledge of God, and bringing into captivity every thought to the obedience of Christ.

Day Thirty-nine
II Corinthians
10:4,5

Isaiah 55:11

So shall God's Word be that goes forth out of _____'s mouth; it shall not return to God void (without producing any effect, useless) but it shall accomplish that which God pleases and purposes, and it shall prosper in the thing for which God sent it.

_____

_____

_____

_____
_____
_____
_____
_____
_____
_____
_____
_____
_____
_____
_____
_____
_____
_____
_____
_____
_____
_____
_____
_____
_____
_____
_____
_____

Day Forty
Isaiah 54:17

But no weapon that is formed against _____ shall prosper, and every tongue that shall rise against (him, her) in judgement _____ shall show to be in the wrong. This (peace, righteousness, security, triumph over opposition) is the heritage of _____, the servant of the Lord, [those in whom the ideal servant of the Lord is reproduced]; this is the righteousness or the vindication which _____ obtains from God ["this is that which I impart to _____ as (his her) justification]."

Journal your thoughts.

_____
_____
_____
_____
_____
_____

Now that you have completed forty days you may want to start over and do it for another forty! However long it takes to get the desired results, it's worth it! So keep praying the Word. Keep speaking what God says about healing, health, and victory over the flesh. Say it until you believe it, not just in your head, but in your heart. Remember, the Bible says in Proverbs 23:7 "For as he thinks in his heart, so is he…" It didn't say what a man thinks in his HEAD! The key is not what you think in your head but rather what you believe IN YOUR HEART!

The way to get something past your head and into your heart is by saying it out loud. Romans 10:17 says, "So faith comes by hearing [what is told], and what is heard comes by the preaching [of the message that came from the lips] of Christ (the Messiah Himself)."

What is the best way to hear the Word? The best way is to hear yourself saying what God says. This will build your faith and shape your heart God's way. Then you will be a man (or woman) after God's own heart!

Don't give up or give in. Stay with God's Word and ultimately you will have what God says; healing, health, and life more abundantly!

Order Form

Books	Price	Qty.
Speak the Word...Salvation	$5.00	_____
Being #1 at Being #2	$10.00	_____
It's Too Soon to Give Up	$8.00	_____
An Angel's Touch	$16.00	_____
For Men Only	$7.00	_____
The Mommy Book	$10.00	_____
A Royal Child	$7.00	_____
You are Somebody	$7.00	_____
A Bright Shining Place	$7.00	_____
Abuse...Breaking the Curse	$5.00	_____
Warriors of the Word (children's illustrated action book)	$5.00	_____

Video/Audio Teaching Tapes

	Price	Qty.
Harvest Time for Your Family (4 videos/5 audios)	$40.00/20.00	_____
Wahoo!Yahu! (1 video, 1 audio)	$15.00/5.00	_____

Poster

	Price	Qty.
Protected (Angels)	$5.00	_____

Music Tapes

	Price	Qty.
New Release — RESTORE! (cassette)	$10.00	_____
Healing in This House! (cassette)	$10.00	_____

Music Tapes (continued)   Price   Qty.

From our Children to You $10.00   _____
(cassette)

Other music tapes available for $5.00 each which include:

Makin' My Dreams Come True   _____
With All My Heart   _____
My Heritage   _____
Living Proof   _____
Music and Ministry   _____
Ain't Nothing Gonna Stop
   You Now   _____
Choose To Be Happy   _____

New Release —
Healing in This House! and
   RESTORE! (CD) $15.00   _____

Other CD's available for $10.00 each which include:

Makin' My Dreams Come True   _____
With All My Heart   _____
My Heritage   _____

For booking information or a more complete listing of all ministry items please contact us at:

*Salem Family Ministries P.O. Box 701287
Tulsa, Ok. 74170 (918) 298-0770
FAX (918) 298-2517*

www.salemfamilyministries.org

Harry and Cheryl Salem

Harry Salem II grew up in Flint, Michigan. After his father's death in 1968 he relocated with his family to Florida. In 1980 he joined Oral Roberts Ministries, and at the age of twenty-six became vice-president of operations, crusade director and director of television production. In his work as author, television writer, producer and director he has won several Angel and Addy Awards. His most powerful and life changing book to men, *For Men Only,* has challenged and changed many men's views on their role in the home and with the Lord.

Cheryl Salem grew up in Choctaw County, Mississippi, and overcame many challenges on her journey to becoming Miss America in 1980. She is an accomplished author, speaker, musician, recording artist and teacher. She has recorded ten albums and CDs and has written numerous books, ranging from her autobiography, *A Bright Shining Place,* to her book to moms on how to pray for your children, *The Mommy Book*.

Together Harry and Cheryl form Salem Family Ministries, which focuses on family. They stress the unity of family, marriage, personal relationships, financial goals and parenting as well as leading motivational meetings on overcoming obstacles, such as abuse, abandonment, poor self-image and financial problems. They have written sixteen books all together, including *An Angel's Touch*, *It's Too Soon to Give Up*, and *Being #1 at Being #2*.

When not in their home in Tulsa, Oklahoma, the Salems continue to minister full-time throughout the world with their children Harry III, and Roman.

"As always, Gabrielle, our true General in the Lord"

Additional copies of this book are
available from your local bookstore.

HARRISON HOUSE
Tulsa, Oklahoma 74153

The Harrison House Vision

Proclaiming the truth and the power Of
the Gospel of Jesus Christ
With excellence;

Challenging Christians to
Live Victoriously,
Grow Spiritually,
Know God intimately.